D1422882

Virgin MoDERN iCoNS

LED ZEPPELIN

Acknowledgements

With very grateful thanks to Philip Dodd, Morse Modaberi,
Helen Johnson and to Michael Heatley,
Northdown Publishing and the staff of the National
Sound Archive for their help in the research of this book.

Tony Horkins is *Melody Maker*'s technical editor as well as a
freelance journalist for publications as varied as *Empire*, *Elle*, *Sky*
and the *Daily Mail*. He has also been editor of the *Virgin Rock
Yearbook*, and in 1996 was part of Goldbug, whose cover version
of Led Zep's 'Whole Lotta Love' reached the UK Top 3.

First published in 1997 by
Virgin Publishing Ltd
332 Ladbroke Grove
London W10 5AH.

Modern Icons conceived and developed
for and with Virgin Publishing Ltd by Flame Tree Publishing,
a part of The Foundry Creative Media Company Limited,
The Long House, Antrobus Road, Chiswick, London W4 5HY.

Modern Icons series © Virgin Publishing Ltd 1997
Text © Flame Tree Publishing.

ISBN 1 85227 673 8

A catalogue record for this book is available from the British Library.

Virgin MoDERN iCoNS

LED ZEPPELIN

Introduction by Tony Horkins

CONTENTS

CONTENTS

INTRODUCTION 10

LIVE AND EXPLOSIVE 22

ROCK'N'ROLL ANIMALS 30

THE AXEMAN COMETH 38

PURE PERCY 46

RHYTHM AND BLUES 54

WHOLE LOTTA LED 62

MUSICAL MOMENTS 70

INFLUENCES 78

THE MUSIC 86

THE HISTORY 88

THE CAST 91

THE BOOKS 92

INTRODUCTION

So what makes an iconic rock figure? The durability of their material? The amount of units they've shifted? A history of impressive chart placings? Well, possibly, but there's no image quite so simply and clearly indicative of a band's iconic status than their ability to be identified in silhouette. And as recognisable as the London skyline, Robert Plant's mane of curly hair and Jimmy Page's laid-back, double-necked guitar swagger were all you needed to know that you were in the presence of the ultimate rock band: Led Zeppelin.

Formed in the late Sixties from the ashes of wannabe icons The Yardbirds and recognisable players on the burgeoning London session scene, Led Zeppelin were always destined for big things. It took just thirty hours of recording and mixing time to pull together a debut album, but its abandoned approach, bone-crunching guitar and ear-shattering vocals set a new standard for the term Heavy Metal.

However it was Led Zep's bending of heavy metal's stiflingly strict rules and regulations that contributed to their longevity. The initial physical package may have been off-the-peg rock circa late Sixties, but the music suggested both an influence and a level of creativity way beyond what was expected of the genre.

That shouldn't have come as too much of a surprise to their record company, Atlantic, who knew they had something a little special on their hands. Which is why they offered the freshly minted band the most substantial deal of the period, a $200,000 advance – enough to put a bustle in anyone's hedgerow. In the Led Zep camp, however, there was never any doubt that they could attract anything but the best and the biggest the industry and its fans could offer. Led Zeppelin only ever thought big.

Before they were even airborne, they'd been busy making their presence known as individuals. Bass player John Paul Jones was already a prominent figure in the airless world of session playing. He'd been picking up regular pay cheques laying a bass foundation for acts as diverse as Marianne Faithfull, PJ Proby, Burt Bacharach, Etta James, Lulu, Tom Jones, Dusty Springfield and the brothers Walker and Everly, cramming in three sessions a day with time to spare for a TV jingle or two.

When Jones wasn't playing bass, his talents were stretched further as an arranger. The original Radio One theme – that was his. Donovan's 'Hurdy Gurdy

Man' and 'Mellow Yellow' and Jeff Beck's 'Hi-Ho Silver Lining' also found their crotchets and quavers in order thanks to a little help from Jones. All this skill, and that was just from the bass player. Led Zeppelin were going to have to find a pretty extraordinary drummer to keep up with him.

Which, of course, they did in the shape of Birmingham-born John Bonham: big man, big drums, big sound. Only twenty-one years old when he joined the fledgling Led Zep, he was too young to have a lengthy, illustrious career behind him, but he'd made enough of a noise backing the little known Tim Rose to attract the attention of Jimmy Page.

Page was quoted as saying he felt Bonham to be the most inventive drummer he'd ever heard, and live and unleashed in Led Zeppelin he proved that he could easily keep up with his more established and experienced new work chums. But for his culpability in inventing the half-hour drum solo, he couldn't put a foot, pedal or stick wrong.

His enormous drum sound and metronomic skills played a critical part in the success of Led Zeppelin. No fan of the controlled studio sound, Bonham threw gaffer tape to the wind and let his drumheads flap free, whether playing them conventionally or, less predictably, with his bare hands.

While his contemporaries fretted about precise microphone positioning and zero room resonance, Bonham was quite happy to thrash away at the bottom of Headley Grange's stately stairway with a single mike hanging off the balcony. The result? A unique sound that guaranteed both him and his band a place in rock's history as innovators.

Led Zeppelin also aquired a reputation as hell raisers. Chucking the TV from the window of your local, friendly Holiday Inn may seem like a rock cliché now, but it took Bonham and co., often with a little help from The Who's Keith Moon, to set the standard. Unfortunately, in more recent times that example has been followed in feeble manner by today's young rockers, who think that dribbling their beer and not making their bed is a strike against the establishment.

Ultimately, however, such excesses took their toll, though it needed more than Bonham's accidental and inevitably drink-related death in September 1980 to silence him, and his sound has lived on. He remains one of the most widely sampled drummers in contemporary music, his inimitable work on 'When The Levee Breaks' continually cropping up as a rhythmic life-saver for dance music producers looking for just a little more swing.

For all their heavy metal histrionics, it was Led Zeppelin's ability to turn a head-banger into a toe-tapper that raised them above the stodgy quagmire of their peers. Not a show band in the traditional sense of the term, it was nevertheless their sheer sense of showmanship that allowed them to stand out from the crowd.

As showy as Bonham's barehanded beating was, it was Jimmy Page's penchant for excessive looking guitars, including his trademark Gibson double-neck, and his occasional desire to trade his plectrum for a violin bow that helped give Led Zep a visual hook in performance.

Along with John Paul Jones, Page had cut his teeth as a session player, backing the likes of The Stones, The Kinks and Donovan, though the great unwashed knew him better as the man who ultimately and confidently replaced both Eric Clapton and Jeff Beck in The Yardbirds.

This was the late Sixties, and soon Page's think-big attitude started pervading the Yardbirds' sound. On their final US tour, they were heard to perform 'I'm Confused', later 'Dazed And Confused', and 'White Summer', which also became part of Zep's repertoire. By the summer of 1968 it was all over for the original Yardbirds, and Page had a decision to make. A ten-day Scandinavian tour with 'The New Yardbirds', or form his own band. Thankfully, the decision came easily. After all, now he was the grand old age of twenty-three.

So he took his low-slung Les Paul and his Marshall stack, turned it up to 11, and re-invented the blues. The world hadn't seen his type or heard his sound before, and suddenly a surfeit of would-be guitar heroes had to find a way to play the guitar as it dangled around their knees.

Not that Page was unable to explore his more sensitive side as a guitar player. But loud rock music and acoustic guitars had never been happy bedfellows, and a surfeit of virtuosity was unheard of in such a basic art form. To begin with this proved all too much for the more simplistic tastes of the American market, and an early US review considered the band to be "loud, impersonal, exhibitionistic, violent and often insane".
What's more, they said it like this might be a *bad* thing . . . .

What the critic hadn't twigged, however, was that Page had a masterplan, and knew exactly how he was shaking up music's aristocracy. And he realised that the success of his mission relied

heavily on the recruitment of the lead vocalist of another Birmingham-based outfit, the less-than-legendary Hobbstweedle. Step forward, Mr Robert Plant.

In fact, Plant didn't just step, he strutted, swaggered and preened while he was at it too. No sooner had he taken to the stage as Led Zep's front man, than he re-defined absolutely what a rock star should look like and sound like. When a spotty, greasy-haired teenager stood in front of the mirror, his fantasy-fuelled mind could metamorphose his hair brush into a microphone and his body into Robert Plant's.

The twenty-one-old singer's lungs had all the power of Bonzo's drum kit, and the bad news was that at one of his first Zep gigs his screaming vocals left the speaker system in tatters. However, the good news was that it just didn't matter. The audience could hear him at the back of the auditorium over the whole group anyway.

And if they couldn't hear, they could gawp. Snakeskin boots, progeny-threatening tight bell-bottomed jeans, flowing open shirt and *that* hair. For the first time, the words 'rock' and 'God' could legitimately be used in the same sentence. And they frequently were.

Keith Moon, or John Entwistle, or possibly both, joked that the combined ensemble would go down like a 'lead Zeppelin', and suddenly a moniker for the approaching mayhem was duly recorded and registered. Now all they had to do was make a record.

After their initial reticence, the Americans lapped up 'Led Zep I's largely blues-fuelled workouts, the Brits jumping on board their star-bound balloon for 'Led Zep II' and its now-legendary inclusion,

'Whole Lotta Love', a million-selling hit single in the US, but never released in Britain. In fact, Zep weren't big on releasing singles, but singalong gems were to be found amongst the lengthy workouts and more than occasional self-indulgences that dominated a lot of their output.

'Led Zep III' gave us 'Immigrant Song'; the

fourth (untitled) album 'Black Dog', 'Rock And Roll' and every music-shop owner's worst nightmare, 'Stairway To Heaven', destined to be massacred whenever an aspiring guitarist asked to test a new guitar. 'Houses Of The Holy' offered 'The Song Remains The Same', 'Physical Graffiti' produced the most expensive album sleeve ever conceived and the truly hypnotic 'Kashmir', 'Houses Of the Holy' and 'Trampled Under Foot'. But although 1976's 'Presence' included 'Achilles Last Stand' and 'Nobody's Fault But Mine', the album – recorded shortly after Plant's near-fatal car crash in Greece – lacked the distinction and direction of previous recordings. Their finest hour had ticked its last and time was moving on.

In late 1976 the band released the soundtrack to one of the most self-indulgent rock movies ever made. 'The Song Remains The

Same', with its bloated workouts of the classics, and the two subsequent albums (including 'Coda', released after Bonham's death), were evidence that Led Zeppelin's glory days had passed.

For the punk movement, Led Zep were an aging anachronism. Upstaged by the new wave, their kind of rock stood as a monument to a time that many wished to forget. Their excesses could only be enjoyed by the privileged, their sound by those not yet tuned in to the tighter, crisper and earthier noise of a new generation. Besides, the new kids on the block couldn't afford the drugs.

And their extravagant tours, the undoubtedly apocryphal stories of hotel orgies involving groupies and various branches of the fish family, the pomp and occasional pomposity, all became the blueprint for an easily parodied image of 'the quintessential rock band'. No one captured that image as tartly or as brilliantly as the 'Spinal Tap' team. When Nigel Tufnell performs his virtuoso guitar solo, using not merely a violin bow on the strings, but producing a

complete violin, the reference was not even thinly disguised.

Although in the later stages, Led Zeppelin, perhaps inevitably, began to lose the focus and direction of their early years, their apparently irresistible rise from 1968 onwards had been masterminded by another iconic figure, the fifth member of the band, manager Peter Grant. Shadowing them like a stalker, Grant was up there with Colonel Tom Parker and Brian Epstein as one of the new breed of celebrity managers, striking, quite literally at times, the fear of the devil into all he crossed, and duly earning his reputation as the fiercest and most feared of rock managers.

Happily encouraging his boys to live life large, he re-drafted the role of the manager by doing exactly the same. He travelled with the band, toured with them and indulged with them. His methods served as a model for all who followed, the opening chapter in the How To Be A Rock Manager handbook.

Grant died in 1995, but his legacy lives on. The influence of the band that he and Page created, and in which every member became a quintessential representative of their particular art, is still to be found in the work of an eclectic mix of newer music makers. Without Zep, would the Eighties have been so kind to rock acts like Def Leppard, AC/DC and Iron Maiden? Would The Cult have sounded quite so raw? Would the Beastie Boys have sounded quite so groovy? Would Frankie have gone to Hollywood, or U2 left Ireland? Would Lenny Kravitz ever have written a song?

Like it or not, the answer's a resounding no . . . .

Tony Horkins

LIVE AND EXPLOSIVE

* *

Led Zeppelin developed their fan base almost entirely through live performance. The band performed rarely on television, gave few interviews, and released no singles at all – by choice – in Britain.

There's only one way a band can function,
and that's on the bloody stage.
Robert Plant

Their current two-hour-plus act is a blitzkrieg of musically perfected hard rock that combines heavy drama with lashings of sex into a formula that can't fail to move the sense and limbs.
Nick Logan, *NME,* 1970

It's just so good to be there to see people flashing back on you. Road fever is the name. It's just total exhilaration – 100% adrenaline.
Robert Plant

You can feel the force of the combined volume hit you physically. It's painful, but it rips out an emotion common to most everyone in the hall. Excitement, and something rude, something so alive it smells.
Roy Hollingworth, *Melody Maker,* 1971

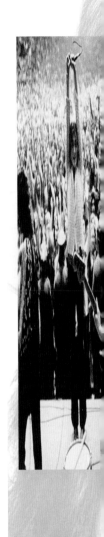

Their live strength was a vital part of their success in the States, a territory their manager Peter Grant decided to concentrate on. Led Zeppelin were the first major UK band to focus their efforts on the US – signing to Atlantic Records, for example – rather than their home market.

Led Zeppelin hit American shores for the first time in late December of 1968 with an awesome fury and a Herculean stamina that even Cream and Hendrix had not prepared anyone for.
Rolling Stone, 1987

Zeppelin started in the States on Boxing Day 1968. Three of the group had never been to America before and didn't know what to expect. My instructions were to go over there and really blast them out. They really did that. Maybe they weren't the greatest thing ever on that first trip, but they got themselves across and the enthusiasm just exploded.
Peter Grant, Led Zeppelin's manager

Before they saw us in America there was a blast of publicity and they heard all about the money being advanced to us by the record company. So the reaction was – 'Ah, a capitalist group'. They realised we weren't when they saw us playing a three hour non-stop show every night.

Jimmy Page,
Melody Maker, 1970

We aren't going to mess around – we're just going to play.

Robert Plant, St Louis, Missouri, 1977

The sheer scale of their shows, their straightforward, hard, bluesy rock, and their position as the most commercially successful act in rock made them an obvious target for punk hostility, as one of the 'dinosaur' supergroups of the mid-Seventies.

Robert Plant came down The Roxy surrounded by millions of bodyguards. I just looked at him, and he's like a real ignorant old northerner, and I felt really sorry for him. Now, how can you respect someone like that?

Johnny Rotten, 1977

Those accusations that were levelled at Zeppelin at the end, during punk, those accusations of remoteness, of playing blind, of having no idea about people or circumstances or reality – there was a lot of substance in what was being said. It hurt at the time, but I'd have to plead guilty.

Robert Plant, *Q* magazine, 1988

Led Zeppelin? I don't need to hear the music – all I have to do is look at one of their album covers and I feel like throwing up.

Paul Simonon, The Clash

I liked the energy of what they were doing, musically, but I didn't pay much attention to what they were saying in the press because I knew that was just a good way of being able to come up with some controversy.

Jimmy Page, 1988

27

*The film, The Song Remains The Same,
released in 1976, the Year of Punk, was an
uneasy marriage of live footage and fantasy
features. It missed the mood of the times, and
was critically panned.*

Far from a monument to Zeppelin's stardom,
The Song Remains The Same is a tribute to
their rapaciousness and inconsideration.
Dave Marsh, *Rolling Stone,* 1976

It's not a great film . . . just a
reasonably honest statement of where
we were at that particular time.
Jimmy Page

The Zep movie is sort of what would have
happened if *Help!* had taken itself seriously as
film noir. And been written and produced,
directed and edited by junior college students
who had just discovered LSD.
Robert Duncan, *Circus*

The most expensive home movie ever made.
Peter Grant, Led Zeppelin's manager

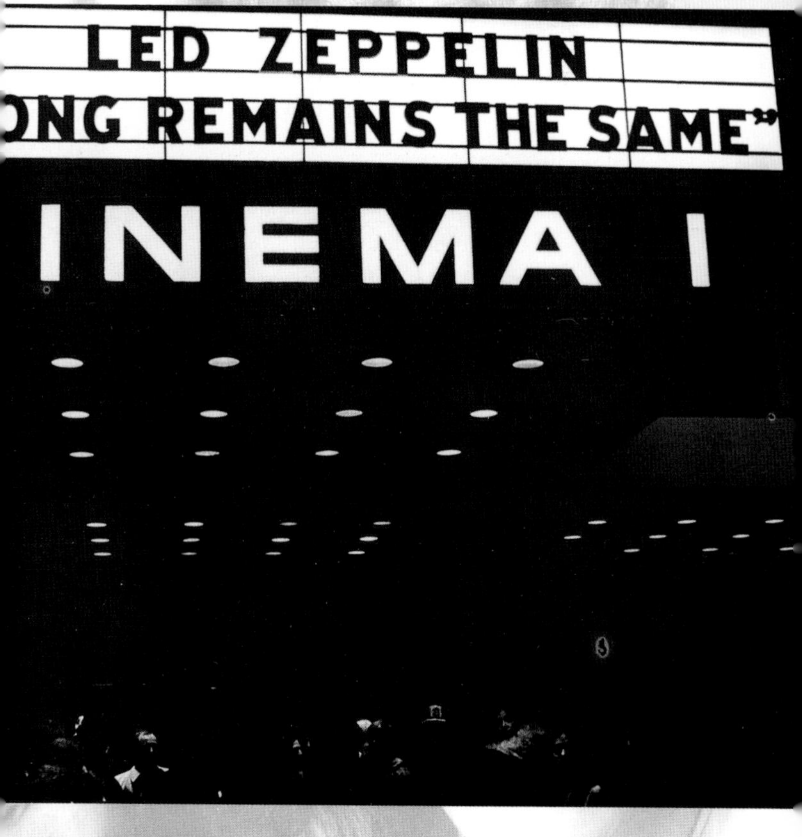
LED ZEPPELIN
NG REMAINS THE SAME”
INEMA I

ROCK'N'ROLL ANIMALS

Since their earliest days on the road in the States, Led Zeppelin have had to deal with a high-profile reputation as outrageous party animals.

You know, it's 1977, and Led Zeppelin have been around for nine years now, and I can't help but wonder if part of their popularity is due to the fact that they're the last of an era of cock rockers who play dirty and, if you'll excuse the expression, 'chauvinistic' rock'n'roll, fulfilling all those wild-hearted bad boy aggressions on stage that this audience only fantasize about.

Jaan Uhelski, *Creem* magazine.

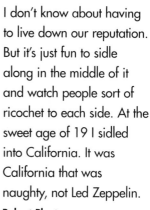

I don't know about having to live down our reputation. But it's just fun to sidle along in the middle of it and watch people sort of ricochet to each side. At the sweet age of 19 I sidled into California. It was California that was naughty, not Led Zeppelin.

Robert Plant

We were in the Midwest and I said something to the hotel clerk about the fact that it must be tough to have all the rock groups in there throwing furniture and TVs out the windows, and he said that they had something worse once . . . and that was the Young Methodists Convention.

Peter Grant

On later American tours, the band would cruise from gig to gig in their private Boeing jetliner 'Starship'. It helped assuage the pain.

You must keep going no matter what happens and that's hard when you're getting on a bit. Touring, though, is a real 1,000 miles an hour speed trip – with that power rush you get of actually performing before large crowds every night – and that's why it's worth carrying on.

Robert Plant, *Creem,* 1974

Down there they've got the richest groupies in the world. Some of the groupies followed our jet in their private jet.

Jimmy Page on Texas

Touring makes you a different person, I think. You always realise it when you come home after a tour. It usually takes weeks to recover after living like an animal for so long.

John Paul Jones

Spinal Tap and The Bad News Thing, they're classic. They really sum up the nightmare aspects of it, everyone can relate to it. Curiously enough there's a bit in Spinal Tap where they can't find the stage and it was very similar to when we were at Madison Square Garden . . . .

Jimmy Page, *Q* magazine, 1988

Semi-official biographies would downplay Zeppelin's on the road activities and the tales of debauchery that have passed into rock legend. In any event, off tour the band went their separate ways.

We never socialised. That's why it lasted so long, I think. We got on the road and everyone was really pleased to see each other. We get back to Heathrow and everyone goes 'Bye!'

John Paul Jones, *Mojo,* 1994

John Paul is the antithesis of a pop star. You never see him. He's like a recluse and only comes out when there's a concert to play or record to make.

Peter Grant, *Daily Mirror,* 1970

35

The ultimate rock'n'roll animal –
in the sense of someone who
understood exactly how the whole
business ticked – was fifth member, the
band's ebullient manager Peter Grant.

I have no musical knowledge, but it's
purely a feeling thing with me. It's not
just liking the sound you hear, it's a
feeling that it's either got the magic or
it hasn't. I can't define it, but it works.

Peter Grant

Grant would say to promoters, Okay,
you want these gigs but we're not
taking what *you* say, we'll tell you what
we want and when you're ready to
discuss it you can call *us*. Peter changed
the rules. He rewrote the book. If we
were the Gods, Grant was The Hammer.

Robert Plant, *Q* magazine, 1988

THE AXEMAN COMETH

Already an established star when Led Zep began, from his session work and Yardbirds days, Jimmy Page's fretmanship alone could have guaranteed him icon status.

I just sort of picked it up. When I was at school I had my guitar confiscated every day. They handed it back to me each afternoon at four o'clock.

Jimmy Page

His acoustic work frightens me sometimes, it is so good. Then I played 'Led Zeppelin Two' and it didn't do anything for me, his electric guitar playing that is. He should really do more acoustic work.

Jeff Beck, *Sounds,* 1971

I just wanted my old partner around for a bit. I wanted to see him swaying around, leaning around so his hair was dangling on the floor. Everyone in the control room was going 'God, look at that man play'. I was sitting there feeling very proud.

Robert Plant on Jimmy Page guesting on Plant's 1988 solo album 'Now And Zen'

Page was not just a talented guitarist, he was a showman, renowned for his onstage virtuosity, and his party piece – playing the guitar with a violin bow.

The Paganini of the Seventies.
Headline in *Melody Maker,* 1970

During 'Dazed And Confused' he grabbed a violin bow, and holding the tip-end about two feet away from the strings, coaxed eerie, shivering riffs from his guitar. He leapt into the air and, using the bow like a fencing foil, precisely hit each string at point-blank range and never missed a beat.
Pillow magazine, 1972

It was suggested to me by one of the violinists in the string section. It obviously looks a bit gimmicky because one hasn't seen it done before, and as soon as you pick up a bow and start playing guitar with it . . . . The fact is it's very musical, it sounds like an orchestra at times.
Jimmy Page

*In performance, his
Les Paul was slung low
as he prowled the stage.*

I chose that Les Paul Custom
purely because it had three
pick-ups and such a good
range of sounds – it seemed
to be the best all-rounder at
the time . . . . Eric must take
the credit for establishing
the 'Les Paul Sound'.
Jimmy Page, *Zigzag,* 1972

It's showmanship. He curls it
all down silent, then barks out
like an electric dog with loads
of sharp bits of bone in his
mouth. He moves well, all the
tricks, sneaking about. It's a
gorgeous action to watch.
Roy Hollingworth,
Melody Maker, 1971

Behind the guitar flashiness was an introverted, private man, the creator of Led Zeppelin's sonic panorama, producer of all the Led Zep albums.

It's just a chord or a riff that inspires me and then I go on and see how it goes colour-wise. The whole thing just grows like an acorn or something.

Jimmy Page, *Disc,* 1970

When I heard Zeppelin, it was like, OK, now I know why I'm not doing well on my classical piano. Because Jimmy Page was the bridge from acoustic to electric music. He showed me what I could do.

Tori Amos, *Q* magazine, 1995

Above all an ambient band, that was the key thing about it.

Jimmy Page, *Q* magazine, 1988

PURE PERCY

Robert Plant – like The Who's Roger Daltrey – was a front man pure and simple. No instrument, just that voice.

His voice had an exceptional and distinctive quality. What amazed me more than anything else, especially after the first LP was finished, was that nothing significant had happened to him before.

Jimmy Page, *Zigzag,* 1973

The blues gave me the freedom to override all pop singers of the era and get up on stage with any group, and my voice started developing at fifteen while I was singing Tommy McLennan numbers. Even now I don't know why it's as powerful as it is.

Robert Plant, *Record Mirror, 1967,* on an early solo release

46

Pretty soul-beater who can do a good spade imitation . . . strained and unconvincing shouting.
John Mendlesohn, *Rolling Stone,* 1969

The trouble was, I could play a lot of different styles but I really didn't know what to do. Sometimes I wanted to do a hard rock thing. At others, a Pentangle type thing. But as soon as I heard Robert Plant, I realised it was likely to be the former.
Jimmy Page

*Plant was the horny
rock god that spotty
teenage boys aspired
to – in their dreams.*

I've been told I'm
a 'sexual beacon'.
Robert Plant

Good to listen to Plant with
his ugly, angry vocals
bellowing to his woman
that he's gonna leave her
right after the next fuck.
Oz review, 1968

If any of my movements
appear sexual then they
are just accessories to the
music at that point in time.
Robert Plant,
Melody Maker, 1977

49

Away from the tours, Plant cultivated a gentle pastoral image.

I think I could sing and shear a few sheep at the same time.

Robert Plant, *NME,* 1974

It gives me room to think, to breathe and live. I wake up in the morning and there are no buses and no traffic. I just revel in these country things. Chickens and goats and me horse. After reading Tolkien I just had to have a place in the country.

Robert Plant

Robert Plant had something of an infatuation with the fantasy figures of English literature, knights and damsels, while Jimmy Page was a fan of occultist Aleister Crowley, buying Crowley's house near Loch Ness, and prompting a media-driven obsession with Zeppelin and the occult that refused to go away.

You see, here I am, the lead singer with Led Zeppelin, and underneath I still enjoy people like Fairport Convention and the Buffalo Springfield. The only heavy band I really dig is the Zeppelin. Apart from that I dig the mellower things.

Robert Plant

He was a huge Celt in those days! I must admit it didn't make much of an impression on Bonzo and I at the time.

John Paul Jones on Robert Plant, *Mojo*, 1994

You can't find anything if you play that song backwards. I know, because I've tried. There's nothing there. We never made a pact with the Devil. The only deal I think we ever made was with some of the girls' High Schools in San Fernando Valley.

Robert Plant on 'Stairway To Heaven', Q magazine, 1988

RHYTHM AND BLUES

At the heart of the Zeppelin sound was Bonzo,
John Bonham, a big man with a big sound. A sound
sampled in later years more than any other drummer's:
Frankie Goes To Hollywood's 'Relax' started the fashion.

Robert suggested I go and check out his
friend John Bonham. When I saw what a
thrasher Bonzo was, I knew he'd be incredible . . .
He was into exactly the same sort of stuff as I was.

Jimmy Page, *Zigzag,* 1972

We always wanted the drums to sound like real drums,
but that hall made them sound like super cannons.

Jimmy Page, on recording Bonham's drums in
the hallway at Headley Grange mansion, Hampshire

That drummer of yours has a
right foot like a pair of castanets.

Jimi Hendrix to **Robert Plant**

Our drummer is amazingly loud.

Jimmy Page, *Melody Maker,* 1969

Bonham's death – he choked in his sleep after a drinking binge – broke the band's heart. They decided not to continue six weeks after he died.

There was a period after he died where
I just didn't touch a guitar for ages.
Jimmy Page

I did nothing for as long as was respectful to
Bonzo, really. Because we *were* best mates.
Rather than take the whole Zeppelin thing and
try and do it myself, I rejected the whole thing.
So I cut my hair off and I never played or
listened to a Zeppelin record for two years.
Robert Plant, 1988

Sometimes at night, when the moon is
high, a mighty thunder is heard in the hills.
Don't be alarmed, the wise ones say, it's only
Bonzo. Doing a soundcheck, in heaven.
Paul Du Noyer, *Q* magazine, 1997

*Alongside Bonham's power and attack,
John Paul Jones contributed his musical and
arranging skills – as well as bass duties,
Jones rounded out the Zeppelin sound on
piano, organ, Mellotron and Moog.*

Organ, in fact, was always my first
love, but for session playing I found it
much easier to carry a bass guitar to
work than a Hammond organ.
John Paul Jones

He comes along to the studio and
he's always got a new instrument to play.
John Bonham, *Melody Maker, 1971*

He asked me if I could use a bass player in
the new group I was forming. Now John Paul
is unquestionably an incredible arranger and
musician – he didn't need me for a job. John
simply wanted to be part of a group of
musicians who could lay down some good
things. I jumped at the chance of getting him.
Jimmy Page

*The Bonham/Jones combination
clicked straight away – from the
very first rehearsals in 1968.*

Bonzo and I connected
immediately, just locked in. Rock
solid and really exciting. Together
we could give Page and Plant the
freedom to go over the top and
add that whole sonic cloud.

John Paul Jones, *Mojo,* 1994

It makes you feel good to hear
Bonham and Jones working
together creating those deep,
surging undercurrents of rhythm
as Page again and again molests
the more vulnerable areas of his
Telecaster.

Felix Dennis, *Oz,* 1968 on the first album

[Jimmy] counted it in, and the
room just exploded.

John Paul Jones on the first
song at the first rehearsal

WHOLE LOTTA LED

* *

Rock solid rhythm, searing guitar, soaring vocals.
The Led Zeppelin sound was the sum of all of its parts.

Everybody in the group is strong. It's not like some groups
where you have one stand-out person and the rest are
passengers. When people see our shows they can come
back again and find out some different facet of our ability.
Jimmy Page

Right from the time Jimmy Page came up to see me in
the Midlands and said he was gonna form this band,
way back in '67, he and I have known that we're such
different characters that we're good for each other.
Robert Plant, *Melody Maker,* 1977

Astrologically it's very powerful indeed. Robert the
perfect front man Leo. John Paul Jones and I are uh
. . . stoic Capricorns (laughs), Bonzo the Gemini. It's
when you are pushing each other to the limits that
the strength of the chemistry comes out.
Jimmy Page, *NME,* 1974

Together on stage, the impact was heightened by the theatrics, including Bonham's flame-circled gong, and his long, long drum solos, a development from the 'Moby Dick' track on 'Led Zeppelin II'.

I really like to yell out when I'm playing. I yell like a bear to give it a boost. I like our act to be like a thunderstorm.

John Bonham

Heard the one about the photographer at Earl's Court whose half-hour allowance fell during Bonham's solitary 40-minute party piece?

Angie Errigo, *NME, 1976*

It's all right when I'm playing.
It only hurts when I stop.

John Bonham, *Melody Maker, 1970*

The power of the Zep sound was the forefather of a later generation of copyists.

If I'm responsible for *this*, in any way, then I am really, *really* embarrassed. It's so orderly and preconceived and bleuurghh. Zeppelin, for all their mistakes and wicked ways, were bigger and greater than any of *that* kind of nonsense.

Robert Plant pointing at a Judas Priest poster, Q magazine, 1988

Listening to Zeppelin albums now, you notice everything the macho metallers haven't been able to photo-copy: complexity, subtlety, idiosyncrasy, vision.

Mark Coleman, *Rolling Stone Album Guide*

The name was a suggestion from Keith Moon or John Entwhistle, who said that Page's plan for a new band would go down like a lead balloon – 'lead zeppelin more like'. Peter Grant suggested the spelling Led to make the pronunciation clearer.

Keith Moon came up with Led Zeppelin sometime during our Yardbirds/the New Yardbirds spell and it seemed to fit the bill; we'd been through all kinds of names, like Mad Dogs, for instance, but eventually it came down to the fact that the name was not really as important as whether or not the music was going to be accepted.

Jimmy Page, *Zigzag,* 1973

MUSICAL MOMENTS

* *

Recorded at breakneck speed, 'Led Zeppelin', the debut album, was a snapshot in time of the first few weeks of the foursome, and the mix of blues and rock they'd tested out on a Scandinavian tour shortly before.

Led Zeppelin – the only way to fly.
Ad slogan for the album

The statement of our first few weeks together is our first album. We cut it in fifteen hours and between us wrote six of the nine tracks.
Jimmy Page

Technical, tasteful, turbulent and torrid.
Melody Maker, 1969

The band's first album was a series of controlled explosions. Hoary blues motifs were pumped up to enormous proportions, clubbed senseless by Bonham's colossal wallop, panicked to distraction by Page's crazed air-raid riffs, pummelled by Jones's slum-demolishing bass lines, and strangled by Plant's lascivious shrieks of lust.
Paul Du Noyer, *Q* magazine, 1987

We took off with so much invigorating energy in '68, and then we curbed that energy so that the whole dynamics of the band would ebb and flow so that we wouldn't burn ourselves out musically by taking the opportunity to go hair-raisingly mad and fade a whole-lotta-loving into the sunset!

Robert Plant,
Melody Maker, 1977

*'Led Zeppelin II'
underlined the band's
arrival as a major force
in rock, going to Number
1 in the UK and US
album charts. Written in
hotel rooms, rehearsed
and recorded on the hoof
amid touring obligations,
the opening track,
'Whole Lotta Love', was
later adopted as Top Of
The Pops's theme music
throughout the Seventies.*

A ragged, nasty projection of male hormonal anguish that's as dangerous if it's feigned as if it's real.
Dave Marsh, *Mojo,* 1994, on 'Whole Lotta Love'

'Whole Lotta Love' is something that I personally need, something I just have to have. We bottle it all up, and when we go onstage we can let it all pour out.
Robert Plant

The famous 'Whole Lotta Love' mix, where everything is going bananas, is a combination of Jimmy and myself just flying around on a small console twiddling every knob known to man.
Engineer **Eddie Kramer**

*On the fourth, untitled, album,
Page and Led Zeppelin unveiled
'Stairway to Heaven' – eight
minutes of music that became the
most requested song on American
FM radio, was played by every
budding music-shop strummer,
inspired a complete album of
cover versions, and took Rolf
Harris back into the charts.*

The music came first. I'd written it
over a long period; the intro fell
into place in Bron-Y-Aur, in the
cottage, and other parts came
together piece by piece. Robert
came out with the lyrics just like
that . . . I'd say he produced 40%
of the lyrics almost immediately.

Jimmy Page, *Zigzag,* 1973

Everybody can interpret them however they will. It's potential optimism, lyrically. It's saying that if you hold tight, you can make it all right.

Robert Plant on the lyrics

They'd come back from the Welsh mountains with this guitar intro and a verse. I literally first heard it in front of a roaring fire in a country manor house.

John Paul Jones

I thought 'Stairway' crystallized the essence of the band. It had everything there and showed the band at its best. It was a milestone for us.

Jimmy Page

75

'Physical Graffiti', the band's first album on their own Swan Song label, went gold and platinum on the first day.

I came up with that title because of the whole thing of graffiti on the album cover and it being a physical statement rather than a written one, because I feel that an awful lot of physical energy is used in producing an album.

Jimmy Page

It's not the kind of music you play before breakfast unless you wake up in a particularly aggressive mood.

NME, 1975

If I'm going to blow my own trumpet about anything I've been connected with, then it would have to be that album.

Robert Plant, *Mojo, 1995*

A work of genius, a superbly performed mixture of styles and influences. They can take as long as they like with the next album: 'Physical Graffiti' will last 18 months or 18 years. And then some.

Melody Maker, 1975

INFLUENCES

*The band's own musical
tastes were diverse.*

Jimmy was into the old rock'n'roll
– Jerry Lee Lewis, Everly Brothers,
Eddie Cochran, big Gene Vincent
fan, and all the rockabilly. And
that Bert Jansch, who was a big
figure for all of us. Very original,
wistful folk music. Robert brought
all the old blues stuff in. And I
brought all the pop stuff and R&B,
which is where Bonzo and I
connected – big James Brown
fans, Bar-Keys and Mar-Keys.
John Paul Jones, *Mojo,* 1994

I suppose if we all sat
down and talked about music,
John Paul and Bonzo and
I simply wouldn't agree at all.
Robert Plant, *Melody Maker,* 1970

*The blues connection was raw
and direct, and sometimes a
little too close for comfort – a
plagiarism suit filed by bluesman
Willie Dixon reached an out-of-
court settlement in 1987.*

I remember a conversation one
night between Jimmy Page and
Mick Jagger. They said 'Between
us, we've had the best of Chess'.
Peter Grant, *Musician* magazine, 1991

'Bring It On Home' was
dedicated to Sonny Boy
Williamson. I should bleeding
well hope so. All Sonny Boy did
was to record that particular
epic Page/Plant composition
back in 1961 – only in those
days it was supposed to have
been written by Willie Dixon.
Charles Shaar Murray, *NME,* 1976

The band's Swan Song label was set up to encourage other acts – they released albums by Bad Company, Dave Edmunds, Maggie Bell – but foundered. In later years, having been extremely unfashionable, Led Zeppelin found their influence working again.

The name Led Zeppelin means a failure, and Swan Song means a last gasp – so why not name our record label that?

Robert Plant, *Rolling Stone*

Led Zeppelin were a great band. I don't know what I was on, barbiturates or something. All I remember is Jimmy Page was wearing red boots.

Chrissie Hynde, *Q* magazine, 1987

I'd like our records to be a mixture of Led Zeppelin, Madonna, the Sisters . . . everything that's ever been good in music. I asked Jimmy Page to produce our next record but he said no.

Wayne Hussey, The Mission, 1987

Led Zeppelin, for most of their fans, and many of their critics, were simply the very definition of a rock'n'roll band.

Led Zeppelin are as much a religion as Scientology, druidism or Manchester United. If you love them you take what they offer with pleasure, and you don't peer for bugs in the bouquet.

Angie Errigo, *NME, 1976*

It's all the stuff of legends now. Greybeards sit around the campfire's glow, and reminisce. Behind them, wide-eyed sprogs stay up – way past their bedtime – just to hear those tales of olden times, when warrior gods walked upon the earth.

Paul Du Noyer,
Q magazine, 1987

THE MUSIC

★★★★★   **Essential listening**
★★★   **OK**
★   **Frankly, not the best!**

Led Zeppelin – January 1969 ★★★
Good Times Bad Times/Babe I'm Gonna Leave You/You Shook Me/Dazed
And Confused/Your Time Is Gonna Come/Black Mountain Side/
Communication Breakdown/I Can't Quit You Baby/How Many More Times

Led Zeppelin II – October 1969 ★★★★
Whole Lotta Love/What Is And What Should Never Be/The Lemon Song/Thank
You/Heartbreaker/Livin' Lovin' Maid
(She's Just A Woman)/Ramble
On/Moby Dick/Bring It On Home

Led Zeppelin III
– October 1970 ★★★★★
Immigrant Song/Friends/Celebration
Day/Since I've Been Loving You/Out
On The Tiles/Gallows Pole/Tangerine/
That's The Way/Bron-Y-Aur Stomp/Hats
Off To (Roy) Harper

Untitled – November 1971 ★★★★★
Black Dog/Rock And Roll/The Battle Of
Evermore/Stairway To Heaven/Misty
Mountain Hop/Four Sticks/Going To
California/When The Levee Breaks

Houses Of The Holy
– March 1973 ★★★

The Song Remains The Same/The Rain Song/Over The Hills And Far Away/The Crunge/Dancing Days/D'Yer Mak'er/No Quarter/The Ocean

Physical Graffiti
– February 1975 ★★★★1/2

Custard Pie/The Rover/In My Time Of Dying/Houses Of The Holy/Trampled Under Foot/Kashmir/In The Light/Bron-Y-Aur/Down By The Seaside/Ten Years Gone/Night Flight/The Wanton Song/Boogie With Stu/Black Country Woman/Sick Again

Presence – March 1976 ★★1/2
Achilles Last Stand/For Your Life/Royal Orleans/Nobody's Fault But Mine/Candy Store Rock/Hots On For Nowhere/Tea For One

The Soundtrack From The Song Remains The Same
– November 1976 ★★

Rock And Roll/Celebration Day/The Song Remains The Same/The Rain Song/Dazed And Confused/No Quarter/Stairway To Heaven/Moby Dick/Whole Lotta Love

In Through The Out Door – August 1979 ★★★
In The Evening/South Bound Saurez/Fool In The Rain/Hot Dog/Carouselambra/All My Love/I'm Gonna Crawl

Coda – November 1982 ★★1/2
We're Gonna Groove/Poor Tom/I Can't Quit You Baby/Walter's Walk/Ozone Baby/Darlene/Bonzo's Montreux/Wearing And Tearing

87

THE HISTORY

Key Dates

July 1968
The Yardbirds split, leaving guitarist Jimmy Page with the name and a tour of Scandinavia to complete. To fulfil the dates, Page eventually recruits Jones, Plant and Bonham. The group does the tour as the New Yardbirds.

October 1968
The group debut as the re-named Led Zeppelin at Surrey University. First album recorded in 36 hours, over two weeks.

November 1968
Act signed to Atlantic Records, with – at the time – the largest ever advance paid to a rock band ($200,000).

December 1968
First tour of the US, supporting Vanilla Fudge and MC5 – start of Zep's huge Stateside success.

January 1969
Debut album goes to US Number 10 – it will reach Number 6 in the UK.

April 1969
First headline tour in the US, a five-week sell-out.

December 1969
'Led Zeppelin II', released in October, reaches to the top of the US album charts and will sell over 6 million units in the States.

September 1970
Band voted Top Group in *Melody Maker* National Pop Poll, finally toppling the Beatles who have been resident in the category for years.

October 1970
Release of 'Led Zeppelin III'. Despite the change to an acoustic feel, the album goes to Number 1 in both the UK and US.

November 1971
The band put out their untitled fourth album, known variously as 'Led Zeppelin IV', 'Four Symbols', 'The Runes' or 'Zoso' after the mystical images on the sleeve. Number 1 in the UK and Number 2 in the US, where it sells some 11 million units.

March1973
'Houses Of the Holy' released – again it hits Number 1 on both sides of the Atlantic.

May 1973
Zeppelin's gig at Tampa Stadium, Florida breaks the US box office record previously held by The Beatles for Shea Stadium in 1965

April 1974
Swan Song, Zeppelin's own label, is formed. It will release all their own future albums, as well as records by Bad Company, Maggie Bell, the Pretty Things and Dave Edmunds.

February 1975
The band's first album on Swan Song, 'Physical Graffiti', again goes on to top both the UK and US charts.

August 1975
Following five sell-out gigs at Earl's Court, London in May, the band are in tax exile. Plant and wife Maureen are seriously injured in a car smash while holidaying in Greece.

March 1976
'Presence' album – inevitably another double Number 1.

October 1976
Film premiere of *The Song Remains The Same*, with soundtrack album released in November, charting at 1 in the UK and 2 in the US.

July 1977
Plant's son Karac dies from a stomach infection while Plant is away on a US tour; remaining dates cancelled, split rumours abound.

June 1979
Zep return to live performance with a European tour.

August 1979
First UK date for four years at Knebworth Festival, playing to over 300,000 fans over two nights. What turns out to be the final studio album 'In Through The Out Door' again goes to Number 1 in the UK and US.

June 1980
Concert in West Germany cancelled when Bonham collapses.

July 1980
What will be Zeppelin's last live concert in West Berlin's Eissporthalle. The final number is 'Whole Lotta Love'.

September 1980
John Bonham found dead at Jimmy Page's home in Windsor.

December 1980
Led Zeppelin issue announcement that they will not continue after Bonham's death.

November 1982
'Coda' released: a selection of unreleased tracks selected by Page and with some overdubs.

July 1985
Three surviving Zeps reform for Live Aid at JFK Stadium with Phil Collins helping out on drums.

January 1986
Band rehearse for a week with Tony Thompson of Chic on drums but decide not to re-form.

May 1988
Zeppelin regroup for Atlantic Records's 40th anniversary bash with Jason Bonham on drums.

October 1994
'Unledded', recorded for MTV's Unplugged series in August, gets series's highest ratings – Plant and Page together, but no Jones.

April 1995
Release of 'Encomium: A Tribute to Led Zeppelin', with various artists including Stone Temple Pilots, 4 Non Blondes, Sheryl Crow, Hootie & The Blowfish, and a duet between Plant and Tori Amos.

THE CAST

John Bonham. Born 31 May 1948, Birmingham. Recommended to Jimmy Page by Robert Plant, Bonham is working the Midlands club circuit with group the Band Of Joy. Renowned for his lengthy drum solos and sheer power – he is now reputedly the most sampled drummer in rock history. Bonham is found dead in his bed on 25 September 1980, after a serious 12-hour drinking bout. Within six weeks, the rest of Led Zeppelin decide not to continue. Bonham's son Jason joins the remaining three to re-form Led Zep at Atlantic Records's 40th anniversary celebrations in 1988.

Peter Grant. Born 1944. Moves into rock management via various odd jobs, some TV and film acting and a career as a wrestler with the sobriquet Count Massimo. Works as tour manager for visiting American artists including Gene Vincent, Chuck Berry and the Everly Brothers, then on to managing the Yardbirds, taking over from Simon Napier-Bell. Learns the ropes in the UK and the States, which determines his strategy for Led Zeppelin and will stand Led Zep in good stead. The fiercest and most feared of rock managers – gets things done with no messing. Also manages Bad Company and Maggie Bell in the Seventies; after Zep split retires to his manor house in Sussex. Dies in 1995.

John Paul Jones. Born John Baldwin 3 June 1946, Sidcup, Kent. An experienced session musician, arranger, and multi-instrumentalist – contacts Jimmy Page when he hears latter is looking for new band members. As a session man, Jones, like Page, had worked with a host of artists, including the Stones (on 'Their Satanic Majesties Request'), Dusty Springfield and Donovan. Takes bass and keyboard role within the band, adding textures with Moog and Mellotron, organ and piano. During time with the band writes and produces Madeleine Bell's album 'Comin' Atcha' (and apparently considers quitting to become choirmaster at Winchester Cathedral in 1973). His subsequent career includes production work for acts ranging from Lenny Kravitz to Heart, REM to Diamanda Galas.

Jimmy Page. Born 9 January 1944, Heston, Middlesex. Before forming Led Zeppelin, is a highly rated and much in demand session guitarist in the early Sixties, recording with, amongst many others, Them, Lulu, The Who and Tom Jones (on 'It's Not Unusual'), and some production, including Nico single 'The Last Mile'. Then joins the Yardbirds in June 1966; when that band splits in July 1968 decides to complete a Scandinavian tour with the New Yardbirds. In his quest for replacement band members the four Zeps come together. Following Led Zeppelin's decision to disband after Bonham's death, Page works in various combinations with musicians including Roy Harper, Paul Rodgers (later in a band called The Firm), David Coverdale, as well as own solo work (album 'The Outrider' in 1988),and the occasional Led Zep/Plant and Page reunions.

Robert Plant. Born 20 August 1948, West Bromwich. Invited to join the New Yardbirds after Page and Peter Grant see him performing in Birmingham band called Hobbstweedle, he has previously been in various local R&B groups, including the Crawlin' King Snakes and Band of Joy, with John Bonham. Has also had two solo singles for CBS released in 1966/67. Post-Zep career highlights include solo albums 'Pictures At Eleven' (1982, reaches US Number 5 and UK Number 2), 'The Principle Of Moments' (1983), part-time R&B outfit the Honeydrippers (line-up includes Page, Jeff Beck and Nile Rodgers of Chic), 'Shaken 'n' Stirred' (1985, including Little Feat's Richie Hayward), 'Now And Zen' (1988), 'Manic Nirvana' (1990), 'Fate Of Nations' (1993), before reunion album with Page 'No Quarter' in 1994.

THE BOOKS

Hammer Of The Gods – Stephen Davis (Pan) 1985
Led Zeppelin – Howard Mylett (Granada) 1976
Led Zeppelin: A Celebration – Dave Lewis (Omnibus) 1991
Led Zeppelin: The Definitive Biography – Ritchie Yorke (Virgin) Updated 1993
Led Zeppelin: In Their Own Words – compiled by Paul Kendall
    & Dave Lewis (Omnibus) updated 1985
Led Zeppelin: A Visual Documentary – Paul Kendall (Omnibus) 1982

PICTURE CREDITS

Pages 2-3 Dick Barnatt. **Page 5** Ian Dickson. **Page 8** Chuck Boyd. **Page 23** Ian Dickson. **Pages 24-5** Chuck Boyd. **Page 27** (t) Dave Ellis; (b) Dick Barnett. **Pages 28-9** Richie Aaron. **Pages 30-1** Chuck Boyd. **Page 33** G. Wiltshire. **Pages 34-5** (t) Fin Costello; (b) Ian Dickson. **Page 37** T. Hanley. **Page 39** Richie Aaron. **Pages 40-1** David Redfern. **Page 42** David Redfern. **Page 43** Chuck Boyd. **Pages 44-5** Chuck Boyd. **Pages 46-7** (l) Ian Dickson; (r) Fin Costello. **Page 48** David Redfern. **Page 49** David Redfern. **Page 50 & 51** Ian Dickson. **Pages 52-3** Chuck Boyd. **Page 55** (l) Chuck Boyd; (r) Richie Aarons. **Page 57** David Redfern. **Page 58** Ian Dickson. **Page 59** Chuck Boyd. **Pages 60-1** Ian Dickson. **Page 63** (t) Dick Barnatt; (b) Richie Aaron. **Page 64** (t) Richie Aaron; (b) David Redfern. **Page 66** Fin Costello. **Page 67** Richie Aaron. **Pages 68 & 69** Ian Dickson. **Page 71** (t) David Redfern; (bl) Chuck Boyd; (br) Courtesy of Atlantic Records. **Page 72** (l) Courtesy of Atlantic Records; (r) David Redfern. **Page 73** John Kirk. **Page 74** Chuck Boyd. **Page 75** Chuck Boyd. **Page 76** David Redfern. **Page 77** Courtesy of Atlantic Records. **Page 78** David Redfern. **Page 79** (t) David Redfern; (m) David Redfern; (b) S. Morley. **Page 80** Chuck Boyd. **Page 82** Mick Hutson. **Pages 82-3** Ebet Roberts. **Page 84** Ian Dickson. **Page 85** Chuck Boyd. **Page 86** Chuck Boyd. **Page 87** John Kirk. **Page 90** Dave Ellis.

All pictures courtesy of Redferns unless otherwise stated.

Every effort has been made to contact copyright holders. If any ommissions do occur the Publisher would be delighted to give full credit in subsequent reprints and editions.